Substitute Handbook

This handbook is designed just for you – to help take the hassle out of those days you can't be at school, whether due to an emergency or a planned absence.

The book is divided into two sections:

Part One – Forms to share schedules and organizational information vital to the smooth operation of your classroom.

Part Two – Forms for your lesson plans and already-done-for-you special day lessons to fall back on when there's no time to plan.

There are lots of ways you can put this book to use. Here's just one suggestion:

- Choose the pages that are appropriate to your needs.
- Make photocopies of these pages.
- Fill in the information as soon as you know it; some can even be done before the new year begins. Consider using pencil so that changes can be made more easily.
- Hole-punch the pages and place in a binder with tabbed sections such as:

   Schedules & Lists
   Procedures
   Lesson Plans
   "Filler-Activities"

- Copy all the worksheets and awards that will be needed to carry out your plans and place them in large, labeled envelopes. Leave the binder and envelopes in an accessible spot.
- Gather all materials – literature books, art supplies, etc., and place them in a container labeled "For the Substitute."

Planning ahead will insure that both your sub and your students experience a successful day. And your return will be a calm and happy one.

If all else fails, ask the kids for help.

What is in this Book?

How can this book help you?

Use the forms in this section to share information a substitute might find helpful when working with your class.

The ideas in this section will help you plan a day for a substitute. These plans can offer your students activities that will insure a positive experience.

Congratulations on your purchase of some of the finest teaching materials in the world.

Author: Joy Evans
Editor: Jo Ellen Moore
Illustrator: Jo Supancich
Cover: Cheryl Kashata

Entire contents copyright ©1995 by EVAN-MOOR CORP.
18 Lower Ragsdale Drive, Monterey, CA 93940-5746

Permission is hereby granted to the individual purchaser to reproduce student materials in this book for non-commercial individual or classroom use only. Permission is not granted for school-wide, or system-wide, reproduction of materials.

Important People to Know at School

Principal: _____

School Secretary: _____

School Nurse: _____

Librarian: _____

Classroom
Assistant: _____

Other Teachers at
this Grade Level: _____

_____

_____

_____

Ask these people
if you are stuck: _____

_____

_____

Custodian: _____

Other: _____

AaBbCcDdEeFfGgHhIiJjKkLIMmNn

School's Daily Schedule

Class begins: _____

Morning Recesses: _____

Lunch: _____

Afternoon Recesses: _____

Dismissal: _____

Lunch Count Procedures and Regulations: _____

_____

_____

_____

_____

School Bus Schedule and Pick-up Areas: _____

_____

_____

Special Procedures

- What to do if a parent wants to pick up a child directly from class:

  _____

  _____

- How to reach the school nurse or office for assistance:

  _____

  _____

- In case of student illness:

  _____

  _____

- Fire Drill Procedure:
  (See school map on page 12 for emergency areas.)

  _____

  _____

  _____

- Other emergency drills:

  _____

  _____

  _____

Students with Special Health Conditions:

  _____

  _____

  _____

  _____

Note to the Teacher: Draw a rough sketch of your class seating arrangement and the names of the students at each area.

Seating Chart

Note to the Teacher: List students alphabetically for easy access. Reproduce this page a second time to list students by special groupings (reading, centers, cooperative groups, etc.).

Class List

Note to the Teacher: Fill in the subject time blocks that you normally follow.

Our Class Instructional Schedule

	Mon.	Tues.
Morning		
Lunch		
Afternoon		

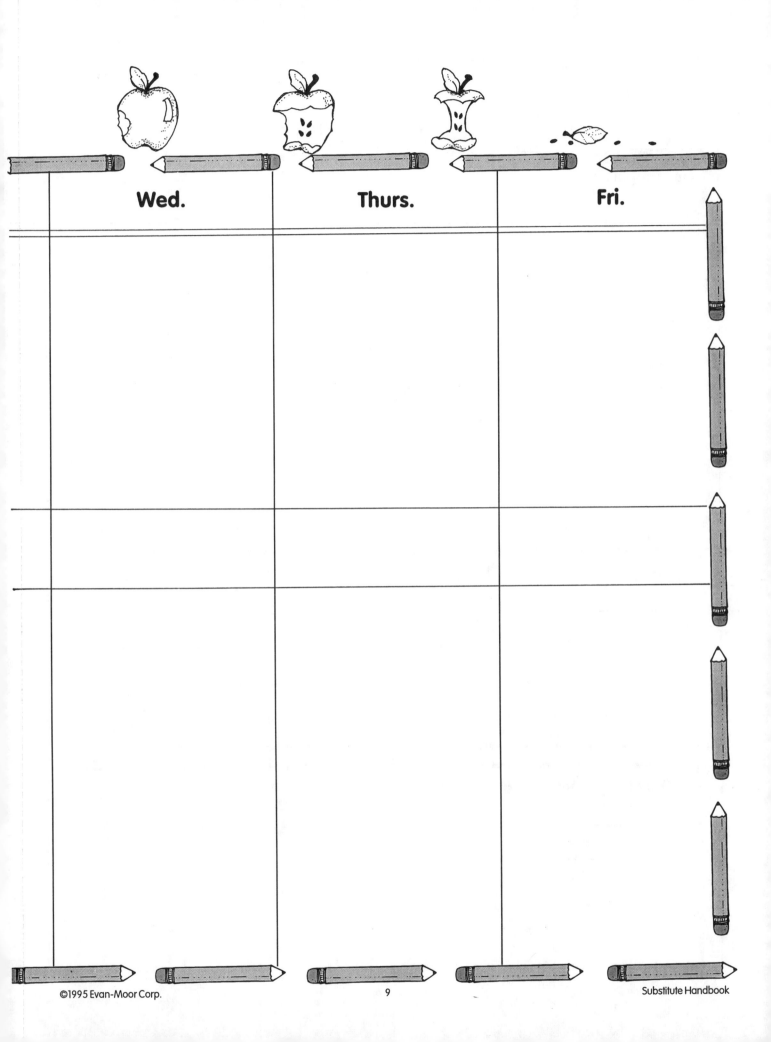

Wed.

Thurs.

Fri.

 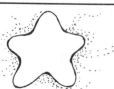

Discipline Plan

General philosophy:

What to do with students that resist positive suggestions for behavior change:

List of appropriate awards and reinforcements:

Rules and Regulations

My kids aren't perfect... but they're working on it.

Classroom Rules:

_____

_____

_____

_____

_____

Hallway Behavior:

_____

_____

_____

_____

_____

Playground Rules:

_____

_____

_____

_____

_____

Note to the Teacher: Make a rough sketch of your school facility and label the major areas.

Map of_____School

Special Students in Our Classroom

The following students are provided with special assistance. List the specialist's name, who goes where, and when.

Time	Specialist's Title/Name	Student Name	Location

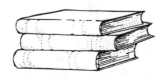

Where to Find It!

Books:

• textbooks

_____

• free reading books

_____

Supplies:

• pencils

_____

• crayons

_____

• construction paper

_____

• scissors

_____

• writing paper

_____

• hand towels

_____

• paste and glue

_____

P.E. Equipment

• balls

_____

• ropes

_____

Where do you go to photocopy?

_____

_____

_____

_____

Special Duties

Before School:

_____

_____

_____

During Recess:

_____

_____

_____

Lunch:

_____

_____

_____

After School:

_____

_____

_____

Note: Reproduce this form and leave with substitute plans.

The Substitute Speaks
Day's Evaluation

Today was.... _____

_____

_____

_____

Next time I would like to.... _____

_____

_____

_____

Things that will require further attention: _____

_____

_____

_____

The best part about today was.... _____

_____

_____

_____

Teaching Ideas and Units to Help Your Substitute

Note to the Teacher: Use this area to plan activities or units that will not be dependent on where you are in a curriculum program. Make this day something someone can step in and offer to your children as a positive learning experience!

Thanks One-Day Sub Plan

Language

Math

_____
_____
_____
_____
_____
_____

Social Studies/Science

_____
_____
_____
_____
_____
_____

Art

_____
_____
_____
_____
_____
_____

Note: Invite students to summarize your day together by writing a letter to their teacher about the day's activities.

_____
date

Dear Teacher,

_____
_____
_____
_____
_____
_____
_____
_____
_____
_____

_____
name

Planning a One-Day Unit for Your Substitute

The following pages provide you with forms to fill out and ideas for short but interesting units. Prepare all the copies and materials and place them in a large envelope ready for the substitute to use.

Primary One-Day Unit – Feline Frolics

This unit offers students the opportunity to spend a day doing activities around the theme of cats. They will do language, math, writing, and art activities. Adapt the lesson to fit the needs of your class. Include whatever literature (fiction and nonfiction) that you have available on this topic.

The drawing lesson on page 24 is a teacher-directed lesson. Students follow along as the teacher does each step on the overhead projector or the chalkboard. Then students may experiment with their own adaptations.

Materials needed to support this unit:
- appropriate literature selections
- the *Pet Survey* form on page 23
- chart paper or a chalkboard
- writing paper
- drawing paper
- pencils and crayons

Intermediate One-Day Unit – Celebrate Colors Day

This unit can be adapted to several grade levels. It provides ideas that could create activities for a day that involves math, language, and art concepts. Students will be actively involved in learning more about a topic they already have some experience with. The emphasis here would be to learn new concepts and develop vocabulary.

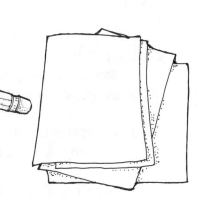

Materials needed to support this unit:
- appropriate literature selections
- chart paper to construct a graph
- writing paper
- *My Color Wheel* form on page 27
- color mixing equipment listed on page 26
- white art paper
- colored construction paper cut to the sizes listed on page 26
- paste or glue

Primary One-Day Unit

Feline Frolics

Share Literature:

Fiction

Millions of Cats by Wanda Gag
Cat Poems by Myra Livingston
Hi, Cat! by Ezra Jack Keats
The Third Story Cat by Leslie Baker
Hot-Air Henry and Cross-Country Cat by Mary Calhoun
Can You Catch Josephine? by Stephane Poulin
Our Cat Flossie by Ruth Brown

Nonfiction

Big Cats and Little Cats and Lions and Tigers by Zoo Books
Cats and Kittens by Rose Hill
The Life of a Cat by Jan Feder
Koko's Kitten by Dr. Francine Paterson
A Cat's Body by Joanna Cole

Discussion Topics:

1. Who has a cat? Tell about your cat: name, size, color, behavior, age, and how you got the cat.

2. Talk about how to care for your cat.

Cat Math:

Create a graph showing the number of cats and other pets owned by your students. Make up word problems that relate the cats to other pets. See page 23.

Crazy Cat Writing

Invite students to make up goofy alliterative sentences about cats.

Materials:
- chart paper for building word lists
- 9" x 12" (23 x 30.5 cm) drawing paper
- crayons or marking pens

Steps to Follow:

1. Brainstorm the names of cats and list them on the board. This may include names of breeds or terms such as tiger, calico, or tabby.

2. The task is to create descriptive sentences using words that begin with the same letter.
   A tiny, tiger cat traveled to Tennessee.

3. Model sentences for the students and then each student chooses one sentence to print on the drawing paper and then illustrates it.

4. Invite students to share their work.

Pet Survey

20
19
18
17
16
15
14
13
12
11
10
9
8
7
6
5
4
3
2
1
0

cat _____ _____ _____ _____ _____

Which is the most popular pet? _____

How many pets are there all together? _____

How many more cats than _____?

Let's Draw Cats